C.R.Gibson®
FINE GIFTS SINCE 1870

All images © Hulton Getty Picture Collection.
Picture research by Jon Wright.
Design by Keith Jackson.
All text, unless otherwise attributed, by Jonathan Bicknell.

Developed by Publishing Services Corporation, Nashville, Tennessee.

Published by C. R. Gibson®
C. R. Gibson® is a registered trademark of Thomas Nelson, Inc.
Nashville, Tennessee 37214
Printed and bound by L. Rex Printing Company Limited, China

ISBN 0-7667-6755-8
UPC 0-82272-46685-2
GB4152

The wonder of fathers

The wonder of fathers

"To follow in your footsteps was all I ever wanted."

"It is a **wise father** who **knows** his own **child**"

– William Shakespeare

"Children.
One is one,
two is fun,
three is a
houseful."

– American Proverb

"Well, it just doesn't get any better than this."

"Honor thy father...
for this is the first
commandment
that comes
with a promise."

"Home is where the heart is."

"As they say:
like
father,
like son."

"To see the **pride** in your **eyes** was good **enough** for me."

18

"But even when
I failed,
I was still good
enough for
you."

"I just couldn't wait for you to come home."

"You helped me feel **big** even when I was little."

"And showed me **how** to care for the things **you** care for."

"To me you were always the best."

"Your arms never **failed** to catch and hold me **tight**."

"For **you** will always be, the one to whom my **first**

words were, 'Daddy, Daddy, Daddy.'"